For the Birds

BIRDS & BLOOMS

For the Birds

Easy-to-make recipes for your feathered friends

The Reader's Digest Association, Inc.
Pleasantville, New York/Montreal

A READER'S DIGEST BOOK

Editor: Barbara Booth
Editorial Intern: Rachel Handler
Designer: Elizabeth Tunnicliffe
Senior Art Director: George McKeon
Executive Editor, Trade Publishing: Dolores York
Manufacturing Manager: Elizabeth Dinda
Associate Publisher, Trade Publishing: Rosanne McManus
President and Publisher, Trade Publishing: Harold Clarke

For the birds : easy-to-make recipes for your feathered friends / from the editors of Birds & bloom.
-- 1st ed.
p. cm.
ISBN 978-1-60652-131-1
1. Birds--Feeding and feeds. 2. Birds--Food. 3. Bird feeders. I. Birds & bloom (Firm)
QL676.5.F597 2010
639.9'78--dc22
2009049987

We are committed to both the quality of our products and the service we provide to our customers. We value your comments, so please feel free to contact us:

The Reader's Digest Association, Inc.
Adult Trade Publishing
Reader's Digest Road
Pleasantville, NY 10570-7000

For more Reader's Digest products and information, visit our website:
www.rd.com (in the United States)
www.readersdigest.ca (in Canada)

Photography credits: Shutterstock Images; iStockphoto; The Reader's Digest Association, Inc./GID

Printed in China
1 3 5 7 9 10 8 6 4 2

NOTE TO OUR READERS
The editors who produced this book have attempted to make the contents as accurate and correct as possible. Illustrations, photographs, and text have been carefully checked. All instructions should be reviewed and understood by the reader before undertaking any project. The directions and designs for the projects in this publication are under copyright. These projects may be reproduced for the reader's personal use or for gifts. Reproduction for sale or profit is forbidden by law.

"A bird doesn't
sing because it
has an answer,
it sings because
it has a song."

—Maya Angelou

Introduction...

It's no surprise that more than 65 million people in the United States feed birds. In fact, bird-feeding has become so popular that over $2 billion dollars is spent on suet and seed each year. And why not? Few other of nature's creatures indulge us by perching right outside our windows. From the red-breasted robins, who scour the lawns looking for earthworms, to kinglets and warblers, who flutter about the foliage looking for insects, to nuthatches and woodpeckers, who cling to tree bark hoping to snag morsels under the bark, birds provide hours of enjoyment all year round. But as much as nature provides, birds are often scrambling to find enough food to feed their young and to fuel their energy during the winter months, when food is scarce. Extend birds a special welcome and they'll be eager to grace your yard all year long.

For the Birds is no seedy bird guide. Inside, you will find 50 quick-and-easy recipes using ingredients right from your kitchen to entice fruit lovers, seed eaters, and suet enthusiasts. In addition, you will be provided with expert advice on feeders, birdbaths, seasonal needs, nuisance critters, and plants and trees birds love. Handy tips offer insight into a number of things that few are aware of when caring for wild birds. And to inspire your creative side while delighting your feathered friends, there are a number of ideas for making homemade feeders using recycled materials, along with several do-it-yourself projects you can complete in an afternoon.

So become one of the millions who enjoy this favorite pastime. Before long you will have hundreds of feathered friends right outside your back door!

attracting birds to your backyard

Providing a backyard sanctuary for birds can be as rewarding for them as it is for you. Just offer them food, water, and shelter and soon your backyard will be brimming with all kinds of winged wonders. Shelter can be in the form of trees, shrubs, or birdhouses; water can be as simple as supplying a birdbath or allowing your hose to drip from a perch for an hour or two; and feeding the birds can be as easy as throwing some bread out the back door or as involved as filling feeders with recipes tailored to the species you want to attract. It's fun, it's satisfying, and it's easy. The most important thing to know is just what will attract your new backyard buddies!

attracting birds to your backyard . . .

What Makes Birds Peck?

Most of the hours in a bird's day are spent finding food to fuel their high-speed metabolism. So if you provide food, they will come—by the hundreds. But if you have a particular guest list in mind for your dinner party, you will need to be a little more conscious of the menu. What they eat depends on the type of bird (see pages 16–17). For example, orioles, mockingbirds, and woodpeckers love fruit, especially oranges; nuthatches, bluebirds, titmice, and Carolina wrens love peanut butter; and nearly all adore soft foods, such as donuts, bread, eggs, pancakes, and cooked pasta. In fact, they will even eat fast food if they happen to come across some littered in, say, a parking lot!

What's more, some birds prefer to dine only on a flat surface, others prefer to perch, and still others hover around a water feeder. And then there's the mockingbird—this territorial bully has a hard time sharing and prefers to dine alone! To satisfy each bird's eating habits, there are several types of feeders, such as tray feeders, suet feeders, water feeders, and seed dispensers. But birds aren't picky about their tableware; many of these feeders can be made from recycled products such as a yogurt cup, soda bottle, or even a Frisbee.

Don't pitch your kitchen scraps!

With hundreds of birds flocking to your feeders each day, you will never be bothered with having to tie up large amounts of waste for trash day. The birds love so many things we don't even think of, like old, wrinkled fruit, fruit peels and rinds, apple cores, cooked potatoes and rice, grated cheese, eggshells, breadcrumbs, and leftover scrambled eggs.

Hearing their song

Now couldn't be a better time to join the 65 million others who have already discovered this rewarding hobby. Pesticides, pollution, and commercial and private development are making it harder for birds to find food and stay healthy. So keep your feeders well stocked and you will be delighted by hundreds of grateful feathered friends beckoning at your back door.

Observing your backyard friends will bring you more rewards than you've ever imagined. You will begin to see that they each have a personality of their own. For instance, orioles stay mostly in the trees, but they love to come out when they see some water to play in. Hummingbirds can hover tirelessly and fly both backward and forward, and they love to eat bugs. Sparrows are always aware that they could be scooped up any minute by a predator, so they hide in low vegetation and then fly at high speeds toward feeders. Nuthatches, named so because they can break open nuts by pecking at them with their sharp beak, can walk up—and down—tree trunks.

These are just a few of the many wild feeder birds that will begin to grace your yard if you keep your feeders well stocked. They will appreciate your generosity and quickly start to depend on you as a primary food source. But don't feel pressured into creating an elaborate sanctuary if that just isn't your thing. If you don't want the bother of putting up feeders, all is not lost: Spreading seed, breadcrumbs, parmesan cheese, and other foods directly on your lawn will still attract cardinals, grosbeaks, doves, sparrows, and many other ground feeders. The key is to keep it easy and fun. The rest is for the birds!

Key Ingredients to Have on Hand

Below are nearly all of the items you will need to make the recipes in this book. You may want to keep this list tacked inside your pantry door—once you begin making these wonderful treats for your backyard friends, they will start to depend on your generosity more and more.

- Raisins, dried cranberries, dates, or currants
- Shelled nuts, peanuts
- Apples, oranges, bananas, watermelon, and dried fruits
- Wild birdseed mix
- Sunflower, safflower, millet
- Lard, bacon fat, rendered suet
- Peanut butter, creamy or crunchy
- Molasses
- Oatmeal, rolled oats
- Stale bread, breadcrumbs, croutons, unsalted crackers
- Cornmeal
- Cream of wheat
- Flour (white or wheat)
- Coarse sand, ground eggshells (for grit)
- Cheese
- Dry cereal
- Dog biscuits (chopped fine)
- Ears of sweet corn
- Vegetable seeds

Do you want to discover the culprits behind your empty feeder or plucked berry bush? Here are the names and brief descriptions of some of the more common wild feeder birds so that you can easily identify and enjoy your favorite avian critters when they come to snack or rest in your backyard haven.

American Robin *Turdus migratorius*

The American robin, despite its name, can be found migrating through all of North America. Both males and females are dark gray, with red-orange bellies, and are approximately 10 inches in length.

Blue Jay *Cyanocitta cristata*

Blue jays, as opposed to bluebirds, are bright blue on the top but have white undersides and a tufted crest on their heads. These are large feeder birds, typically between 10 and 12 inches, and are most well known for their loud and varied birdcalls.

Chickadee *Poecile*

Though there are several familiar varieties of feeder chickadees spanning the northernmost parts of North America (such as the black-capped, boreal, mountain, and Carolina chickadee), they share many of the same physical characteristics; these include a tiny size of between 4 and 5½ inches, in addition to gray/black/brown wings, crown, back, and throat area, with white belly and eye patches.

Dark-Eyed Junco *Junco hyemalis*

Dark-eyed junco's span North America and are sometimes known as the "snowbird," marked specifically by their white outer tail feathers. These birds are small, only 5–6 inches in length, and typically satiate themselves on weeds growing in winter gardens.

Evening Grosbeak *Coccothraustes vespertinus*

Of all grosbeaks, the evening grosbeaks visit the feeder most frequently. Their bodies are bright or pale yellow, and they have dark wings, grayish brown heads, and unusually large beaks for their 7–8-inch bodies.

Finch *Carpodacus*

The three most common feeder finches are house, purple, and goldfinches. These small social birds are about 5 inches long and are prevalent throughout North America. Of each variety, females are usually brownish and lighter in color than the male finches.

Mourning Dove *Zenaida macroura*

Another large feeder bird, the 10–12-inch-long mourning dove is recognized by its melancholy call and can be found throughout North American farms, suburbs, and woodlands. The mourning dove has a slim brown body, black-tipped wings, and randomly placed black spots.

Northern Cardinal *Cardinalis*

A well-recognized wild feeder bird, cardinals are found up and down the Eastern Coast sporting their flashy red coats and bills. The male cardinals are all red with a black throat, while the females are brownish yellow, with red beaks, wings, and tails. Northern cardinals have crested heads and are between 7–8 inches in length.

Nuthatch *Sitta*

The red or white-breasted nuthatches received their name for their peculiar way of wheedling their beaks into nuts while eating. They can be found walking headfirst down trees, with blue-gray bodies and white throats. A red-breasted nuthatch is tiny, only 4 inches long, with a red belly; the white-breasted nuthatch has a mostly white underside and is larger, between 5–6 inches long.

Red-Winged Blackbird *Agelaius phoeniceus*

Male blackbirds are full black from head to tail, with a patch of red-and-yellow striping across the wing; the females are tan, with a brown striped pattern spanning the length of their bodies. The birds range all over North America and grow to approximately 8 inches.

Sparrow *Zonotrichia*

There are numerous types of sparrows, but the most likely candidates found at feeders in North America include song, tree, house, and white-throated sparrows. Sparrows are generally brown in body with light or gray bellies and white- and black-striped eye patches. Measuring between 5 and 7 inches long, sparrows are distinguished easily by their varying songs.

Towhee *Pipolo*

Wild feeder towhees are between 7 and 8 inches and can either be Eastern or spotted towhees, both sharing dark heads and bodies and dark red flanks. Spotted towhees have white-tipped feathers, giving the bird a speckled appearance.

Tuffed Titmouse *Parus bicolor*

Titmice are about 5½ inches long, with bluish gray bodies and pale undersides. They are named for the tufts of feathers on their head and are mostly found in eastern North America.

Woodpecker *Picoides*

Both the downy and hairy woodpeckers are frequent visitors of birdfeeders. The hairy woodpecker is about 1½ inches larger than the typical 5-inch downy woodpecker and with nearly identical plumage. Both are black with white-striped cheeks and eye patches, white bellies, and spots. The most distinguishing marking of a woodpecker, however, is the small patch of red on the head feathers.

Food Birds Love . . .

From Your Refrigerator or Pantry	Who Finds Them Irresistible
Bread, pancakes, muffins, donuts, cornbread, graham crackers	Wrens, mockingbirds, thrashers, sparrows, warblers, tanagers, titmice, towhees, creepers, robins, blackbirds, kinglets, cardinals, grosbeaks, buntings, chickadees, bluebirds, thrushes, starlings, nuthatches, catbirds
Suet rendered from beef fat	Woodpeckers, wrens, warblers, tanagers, nuthatches, creepers, chickadees, orioles, titmice, mockingbirds, cardinals, goldfinches, bluebirds, grosbeaks, buntings
Peanut butter	Towhees, goldfinches, cardinals, chickadees, wrens, sparrows, titmice, grosbeaks, buntings, juncos, blackbirds, woodpeckers
Berries	Waxwings, robins, bluebirds, thrushes
Raisins and currants	Waxwings, orioles, robins, bluebirds, thrushes

From Your Refrigerator or Pantry	Who Finds Them Irresistible
Nuts	Creepers, towhees, juncos, thrashers, mockingbirds, warblers, woodpeckers
Apples	Waxwings, mockingbirds, thrashers, wrens, cardinals, grosbeaks, buntings
Bananas, grapes, oranges, watermelon, cherries, cantaloupe	Tanagers, orioles, woodpeckers, mockingbirds, thrashers, warblers, cardinals, grosbeaks, buntings, goldfinches, finches, waxwings, catbirds

Foods that HARM . . .

Although it seems that birds will eat just about anything, there are a few foods that you should never offer to your feathered friends. Here are some that could put them at risk.

Salt and salty foods, such as peanuts, corn chips, and potato chips

Uncooked rice • Dried peas, beans, and lentils

NOTE: To find out which seed a particular bird prefers, see "Types of Seed and the Birds They Attract" on pages 32–33.

seeds and suets

The first food we think of when it comes to feeding birds is seed. There are so many kinds to consider—from cracked corn and white millet to milo, sunflower, and thistle—that it can seem overwhelming. If you're feeding a crowd, you want seed that appeals to a lot of different birds. Sunflower and millet will do the trick for most, but to attract the more unusual birds, you'll want to include safflower seeds.

Suet is an excellent source for fueling the birds' high-speed metabolism and is the food of choice for many, especially woodpeckers, nuthatches, chickadees, and jays. To encourage the fruit and nut eaters, mix in peanut butter, raisins, cranberries, and currants.

simple seed snacks . . .

Backyard Basic

A proven backyard success, this birdseed recipe leaves nothing to be desired.

- 1 cup black-oil sunflower seeds
- 1¼ cup stripped sunflower seeds
- ½ cup sunflower hearts
- ½ cup millet
- ½ cup dried corn
- ¼ cup safflower seeds

Mix all ingredients together and serve in a hanging tube feeder, hopper feeder, or lay out on a tray feeder.

Yields: 5 cups
Attracts: General birds

A little birdie told me . . .

The seed that attracts the widest variety of birds is sunflower. The black-oil sunflower seed contains a kernel with a very high fat content, which is ideal for most winter birds. It also has a thinner shell that is easier to crack than the striped sunflower seed.

A little birdie told me . . .

A calcium-rich diet is essential for birds so that they can produce healthy eggs, but oftentimes it's hard for them to find a viable source. Adding ground-up eggshells to their food will provide nourishment and aid their digestion.

Calcium Feast

Next time you cook eggs, save the shells for a calcium-rich bird treat.

3 cups wild birdseed or homemade seed mix
3–5 eggs (shells only)

Rinse the shells and put them on a cookie sheet to bake at 350°F (177°C) until dry. • Use a rolling pin or spoon to crush them into fine pieces and sprinkle them into your seed mixture. • Fill a tube feeder with this calcium-enhanced seed or serve in a tray feeder.

Yields: 3 cups
Attracts: General birds

Carrot Seed Mix

Carrots add a unique flavor to this birdseed recipe.

2 carrots, grated
2 cups wild birdseed or homemade seed mix
½ tsp. cayenne pepper

Mix together the grated carrots and birdseed in a medium-sized bowl. • Sprinkle the cayenne over the seed mix and stir. • Serve in any tray, hopper, or tube feeder.

Yields: 2 cups
Attracts: General birds

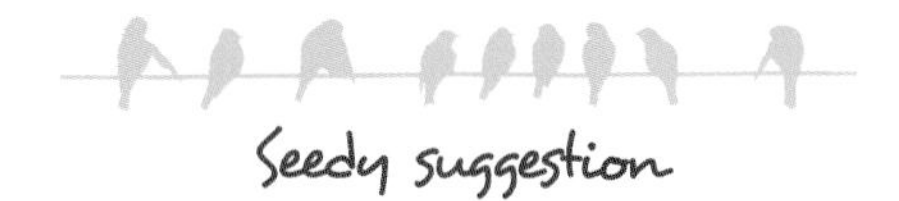

Seedy suggestion

To keep sunflower seeds that fall to the ground from sprouting, bake them in the oven for 20 minutes at 250°F (121°C) before filling your feeders.

A little birdie told me . . .

Ground-feeding birds will be especially grateful if you shovel or stamp down the snow around your feeders so that they can get at the spilled-over seed.

Seed Blocks

These seed blocks can be made into any shape, depending on your choice of container. Thrashers, woodpeckers, and finches especially love them.

1 oz. unflavored gelatin
¼ cup water
1 cup wild birdseed or homemade seed mix
small, empty plastic container
(such as a margarine tub)
mesh bag or metal suet cage

Dissolve 1 oz. of unflavored gelatin in ¼ cup of water in a small saucepan by stirring over low heat until water is clear. • Remove from heat and then stir in 1 cup of birdseed and mix well so that all the seed is coated with gelatin. • Pack mixture firmly into a plastic container and chill in the freezer until solid. • Remove from container, slice, and serve in a mesh bag (the kind potatoes and onions come in), or slice and serve in a metal suet cage.

Yields: 1 seed block
Attracts: General birds

A little birdie told me . . .

Birds must constantly replenish their grit intake, so keep a bowl of sand outside by your feeders. Children's play sand is too fine for birds. Instead, opt for river sand, which is ideal because of its large grain size.

Sand and Seed

This homemade seed mix of familiar favorites is sure to please all of your backyard guests.

3 cups sunflower seed
3 cups millet
2 cups hempseed
1 cup canary seed
1 cup soybean seeds
½ cup sand

Mix everything evenly in a large bowl and serve in a tray, hopper, or tube feeder.

Yields: 10 cups
Attracts: General birds

Graham Cracker Grit

This is a meal that birds can really sink their beaks into.

- 1 cup wild birdseed or homemade seed mix
- 1 cup breadcrumbs
- 1 cup graham cracker crumbs
- 1 cup melted suet
- 2 tsp. sand (for grit)

Combine all ingredients in a large bowl and mix together thoroughly. • Serve on a tray feeder.

Yields: 4 cups
Attracts: General birds

A little birdie told me...

Creating your own birdseed mixes can save you money by eliminating wasteful "filler" seeds found in store-bought mixes that birds often ignore or toss out.

Cornmeal Flaxseed Crumble

Sprinkle these crumbs onto a tray feeder or on the ground and watch the birds hurry in to feast.

- 2 cups cooking grease
- 5 cups cornmeal
- 1 cup flaxseed
- 2 cups flour
- 1 cup barley
- 2 or 3 eggs
- 1–2 cups milk or water

First fold all the ingredients together in a large bowl and thin with the milk or water (either will work equally well) to create the consistency of cake dough. • Using a large spoon, spread the entire mixture onto shallow baking sheets and bake at 350°F (177°C) for 30–40 minutes until hard. • Let cool, remove from the baking sheets, and crumble onto a tray feeder or on the ground in your yard.

Yields: 10 cups
Attracts: General birds

A little birdie told me . . .

It is best to store seed in an airtight container so that insects and mice don't find their way into the bag.

A little birdie told me . . .

When buying seed, make sure the seed inside the bag is not dusty and does not smell moldy or stick together in clumps. This is an indication that the seed is old.

Birdseed Wreath

This wreath can hang outdoors any time of year. Just change the ribbon to match the season.

- 1 oz. unflavored gelatin
- 1 cup water
- ½ cup black-oil sunflower seed
- ½ cup safflower seed

Combine unflavored gelatin with water over low heat and stir until gelatin is dissolved. • Remove from heat, pour in seed, and mix well until seed is entirely coated with the gelatin mixture. • Form into a wreath and chill in the freezer until solid. • Loop a ribbon through the hole and hang from a tree.

Yields: 1 wreath
Attracts: General birds

Sprouted Millet

Birds love millet seed, and taking the time to sprout your own millet is fun and a special treat for the birds.

1 cup millet sprigs

Take a large freezer bag and line it with paper towels to block some of the light. • Place the millet sprigs in the bag and use a spray bottle to wet them completely. • Seal the bag and keep in a dark place, spraying the sprigs with water a few times a day until they sprout. • When sprouted, remove the paper towels and set the bag in a sunny spot until the leaves turn green. Serve on a tray feeder.

Yields: 1 cup sprouts
Attracts: Buntings, Carolina wrens, doves, finches, juncos, pheasants, quail, siskins, sparrows, towhees, thrushes

Grow a millet garden

Millet is an annual grass that is simple to grow. A crop will mature in just 6–10 weeks after planting seeds and will continue through the fall. Your birds will love it!

Types of Seed and the Birds They Attract . . .

Bird	Seed
Blackbird	Buckwheat, canary, millet, oats, sunflower, thistle, whole or cracked corn
Blue Jay	Hemp, melon, safflower, sunflower, whole or cracked corn
Cardinal	Buckwheat, cracked corn, millet, milo, sunflower
Chickadee	Canary, hemp, melon, oats, pumpkin, squash, sunflower, thistle, whole or cracked corn
Finch	Canary, cracked corn, milo, sunflower, thistle, white proso millet
Grosbeak	Apple seeds, cracked corn, melon, millet, peanuts, soybeans, sunflower
Junco	Canary, cracked corn, hemp, peanuts, pumpkin, squash, sunflower, thistle, white proso millet

Bird	Seed
Mourning Dove	Cracked corn, milo, millet, peanuts, sunflower, thistle
Nuthatch	Cantaloupe, melon, peanuts, sunflower
Robin	Cracked corn, peanuts, sunflower
Sparrow	Cracked corn, millet, milo, peanuts, sunflower seeds
Titmouse	Canary, cracked corn, peanuts, safflower, sunflower, thistle
Towhee	Barley, canary, cracked corn, hemp, millet, milo, oats, thistle, sunflower
Woodpecker	Cracked corn, peanuts, sunflower

Birds don't need fancy, complicated feeders. They'll be happy to eat out of just about anything that holds their favorite food. In just minutes you can create simple but clever functional feeders using items you have at home.

Cupcake Pan Bird Platform

Feeders with compartments are an excellent source for displaying a smorgasbord of goodies for your feathered friends. Use an old cupcake pan or muffin tin and fill each compartment with a different seed, or add peanuts, raisins, and cranberries. The sky's the limit. Secure the pan onto a pole so that it sits about 5 feet up from the ground. Plastic egg trays or ice trays also work!

Milk Jug Feeder

This is a simple project that can be completed in about 15 minutes. To make, thoroughly wash a half-gallon milk container. With the cap off, wrap a long, thin wire around the top of the jug and replace the cap to keep the wire secure. This wire will be used for hanging the jug from a tree branch. On each of the two sides opposite the handle, cut a large hole, about 4 inches in diameter, leaving room beneath each hole so that you can crisscross two 12-inch dowels through the sides for perches. Fill with seed, sit back, and watch the birds enjoy their new feeding station.

You can also use laundry detergent jugs. Tie a string around the jug's handle for hanging, cut a large single hole opposite the handle, and fill with seed.

Hanging Egg Carton Feeder

This works on the same notion as the cupcake pan but is hung from a tree rather than displayed on a pole, like a table. To assemble, cut off the lid and punch holes in all four corners of the egg carton. Thread a 30-inch piece of yarn or string through each hole and then gather all four strings together at the top and tie all of them into one large knot so that you can hang the carton from a tree. Fill each compartment with seed or other treats.

Terra-Cotta Ground Feeder

These terra-cotta flowerpots make an excellent ground feeder. Simply place one pot upside down and the other on top, filled with sand or rocks to keep it in place. Then place a large saucer on top to serve as the tray. Saucers can also sit atop tree stumps and rock walls.

Orange Suet Ball

Give the birds an extra-special treat with a decorative suet ball. Make your favorite suet recipe (see pages 43–55) and fill an orange half. Insert sticks for perches and use a little string for hanging from a tree.

Tray Feeders . . .

A tray feeder, also called a platform feeder, is the easiest and most versatile way to provide food in your backyard, and it will attract the greatest number and variety of feeder birds, including buntings, cardinals, chickadees, finches, nuthatches, sparrows, doves, and titmice.

- You can also put almost anything in a tray feeder—from nuts, fruit, and seed to suet and even leftover scrambled eggs.

- Tray feeders can be bought or made using either solid wood lumber or heavy plastic. To make the birds more comfortable and therefore more likely to visit the feeder, the tray should be shallow and mounted about 5 feet off the ground on a wooden, metal, or plastic pole (again, this can be made or purchased). It can also be hung (see opposite page) or placed on a high stump. The advantage of a tray feeder is that it displays the seeds openly, attracting many birds to the feeder. In addition, trays accommodate several birds at a time, allowing even the more timid birds to feed freely.

- Birds love to perch on its ledges, and many different types of birds will feel comfortable sharing such a wide tray—even the territorial woodpecker! What's more, tray feeders inevitably become two-tiered feeders, the ground serving as a second station, where ground feeders such as juncos and quail will snack on the seed scattered from the tray.

- There are some downsides to tray feeders that you should be aware of, though: bad weather and unwanted visitors, such as squirrels and deer. To prohibit food from getting blown away or steeped in rain, it is important to equip the feeder with a clear cover to keep the feed stable and dry while ensuring that it is still visible to the birds. As for those pesky critters, you could put a baffle on the pole, mix red pepper in the seed, or try some of the other solutions mentioned on pages 38 and 39.

Tray Feeder Project . . .

Tray feeders are one of the most popular options for attracting backyard birds. Here's a way to build your own for less than $10!

1. Glue the four pieces of cedar together to make a square box.
2. Hammer in two 1½-inch panel nails at each intersection to reinforce the glue.
3. Determine which side is the top. Place the frame bottom-side-up on your work surface, then center the aluminum screen on top.
4. Place the molding strips on top of the screen, again forming a box, overlapping the joints of the feeder to add strength.
5. Hammer four of the 1-inch panel nails, evenly spaced, along each side to secure the molding and screen to the base of the feeder.
6. Turn feeder over so the screen is closest to your work surface. With a ruler, find the center of each side and mark it with a pencil.
7. Using a 1⁄16-inch drill bit, drill a pilot hole no deeper than ¼ inch in the center of each side. Screw in the eye screw to each side using the pilot holes.
8. Attach one 10-inch length of chain to each eye screw, using the pliers to open and close the links.
9. Attach the end of each 10-inch chain to the larger link to make the hanger. Then hang and wait for your feathered friends to arrive!

Materials

4 pieces of rough cedar, cut to 15⁄16 x 2 x 9 1⁄16 inches
4 pieces of molding strips, cut to ½ x ¾ x 9 ¼ inches
1 10 x 10-inch piece of aluminum screen
8 1½-inch panel nails
16 1-inch panel nails
4 8mm or ½-inch eye screws
4 10-inch-long pieces of No. 16 jack chain
1 ¼-inch-long link of chain (for hanging plants)
Exterior wood glue
Ruler
Needle-nose pliers
Hammer
Drill with 1⁄16-inch drill bit

Keeping Unwanted Visitors at Bay . . .

No matter how resourceful you are, sooner or later you will have to resign yourself to the fact that squirrels and other pesky critters are going to sample your offerings. Let's face it: Squirrels, deer, raccoons, and, depending on where you live, even bears need to forage for food in order to survive, just as birds do. And if you're putting food out there, they will gladly come to dine.

So you have two options: You can either welcome them and be entertained by their silly antics, or you can find ways to outsmart them. Here are some ingenious methods that people have come up with over the years to keep these unwanted visitors at bay.

- **Feed them!** Put out some dried ears of corn on spikes or sprinkle bread and cracked corn in an area far away from your feeders. This will create a diversion.

- **Keep feeders away from jumping-off points.** Squirrels not only climb, they leap! Make sure you place your feeder at least 10 feet away from trees or eaves or other things from which a squirrel can jump and land on your feeder.

- **Purchase squirrel-proof feeders.** There are feeders designed to keep squirrels and other critters away. Some come with a weight-sensitive device that closes the feeding port when a heavy object stands on it. Others come with perches that tilt downward when a squirrel lands on them, causing the squirrel to fall to the ground.

- **Use squirrel baffles.** On pole-mounted feeders, place a cone-shaped metal baffle about 4 feet up the pole so squirrels and raccoons can't climb up. Dome-shaped baffles can be placed over the feeders so squirrels slip off.

- **Don't let them cross the line.** Hang feeders from a clothesline or wire between two trees and thread soda bottles, tin cans, empty spools of thread, milk jugs, or anything else that will spin and cause a squirrel to lose its footing. It's also a great source of entertainment as you watch squirrels try to cross the line!

Hang a Slinky. Yes, that much-loved children's toy. Thread a feeder post through the Slinky, attach one end under the feeder, and let it drape down the post. Shorten the Slinky if it touches the ground.

Spice it up. Add cayenne pepper or chili pepper to mixes and suets (see Squirrel-Beater Suet and Spicy Peanut Seed, pages 55 and 96). The birds can't taste or smell it, but the squirrels find it offensive and run for cover.

Put up a fence. If deer, raccoons, and other larger mammals are a nuisance, put a fence around your feeding area.

Take 'em indoors. If larger mammals seem to be a problem, take your feeders in for a week or two. They will have to leave your yard and go somewhere else to find a food source. It will be quite a while before they come back to bother you and your feathered friends.

Seed Dispensers . . .

Seed dispensers are ideal because they can hold a lot of seed, shelter the seed from the weather, and distribute the food on a need-to-have basis. Because of this, you aren't constantly trudging to the feeders for a refill. The two most well known types of seed dispensers are the tube and hopper. Each has its advantages, but they are limited when it comes to attracting a large number of birds. One is more tailored to small birds, while the other serves a variety of species but has limited space. To attract the largest number of birds and the greatest variety, it is always best to offer several types of feeders in your yard.

Tube Feeder

- Tube feeders are ideal for smaller birds that love seed, because they can feed without getting pushed away by the more aggressive, larger birds. That's because the perches are too small for the larger birds to hold on to. And that means it's off-limits to squirrels, too!

- Because birds can pull out only one or two seeds at a time, the tube feeder stays full for weeks, saving you time and money in the long run, and that's a big consideration when you provide for hundreds of backyard visitors each day.

- Tube feeders were at one time designed to hold only the smallest types of seed, particularly thistle, which is more costly than most, but now the feeders are designed to accommodate larger seeds. They can even be filled with nuts if you choose. But there's no need to limit yourself to just one tube feeder in your yard; if you want to offer a variety of seeds, hang several tube feeders, or else purchase a tube feeder that has multiple tubes so you can provide a variety of seeds inside separate compartments within the same tube. Thistle is one of the more popular seeds for a tube feeder, which is a favorite among purple, house, and goldfinches.

- Tube feeders are weather-proof and are generally made from both metal and plastic, which expose a single seed. Others are made of wire mesh.

Hopper

- Like tube feeders, seed lasts for a long time in a hopper feeder, so there's no need to trudge to your feeder daily to refill. The hopper feeder has a built-in storage unit that automatically releases seed when there's none left on the tray. That way, you can be rest assured that your feathered friends are getting fresh seed when they need it, especially if you are away.

- You will find hopper feeders in many sizes. Some are small and lightweight; others are huge and made of metal or wood. Some of these larger ones can even store up to 10 pounds of seed! And it doesn't matter what type of seed—it takes any kind, including nuts.

- Another advantage of the hopper feeder is that it accommodates a large variety of birds because they are able to perch on the tray. However, there isn't much room for a lot of birds at one sitting, like a tray, or platform, feeder offers (see page 36).

beak-smacking suets . . .

Bluebird Miracle Meal

When cooled, this mixture becomes hard and can be cut into chunks resembling fudge! Feel free to introduce a little variety by adding raisins, sunflower hearts, and mealworms.

1 cup lard or melted beef suet
1 tsp. corn oil
4 cups yellow cornmeal
1 cup all-purpose flour

In a large saucepan, melt the suet over low heat. • Remove the pan from heat and stir in the other ingredients. • After the mixture cools and becomes hard, cut it into chunks and serve in a suet feeder or as slices on a tray feeder.

Yields: 2 large suet molds or 10 slices of suet
Attracts: General birds

Mealworms to go

You can purchase mealworms online, from a catalogue, or at a pet store.

Fly spy

Suet is excellent for nestlings and fledglings because it is so soft. If a bird takes a sampling of fat and flies away with it in its beak, watch where it goes; you may come across a nest full of adorable hungry babies.

Cardinal Casserole

A backyard favorite for more than just cardinals.

- 1 cup cornmeal
- 1 cup rolled oats
- ½ cup bacon grease
- 1 cup flour
- 3 tbsp. dried milk
- ½ cup breadcrumbs
- 1 cup water
- ½ tsp. baking soda
- empty 1-pound coffee can

In a medium to large mixing bowl, combine the cornmeal, oats, and flour. • Add in the bacon grease and dried milk. Sprinkle in the breadcrumbs. • Slowly pour in the water and mix well. • Then add the baking soda and mix together a final time. • Bake in the oven for an hour inside a 1-pound coffee can at 350°F (177°C). • After it has cooled, cut the "casserole" to fit into your suet feeder. You can also bake this mixture in small foil tins.

Yields: 1 coffee can or 1–2 foil tins

Attracts: A variety of birds, especially bluebirds, cardinals, Carolina wrens, crows, ravens, starlings, and woodpeckers

Eggshell Suet

The entire cup of ground eggshell in this suet mix provides much needed calcium for feeder birds.

- 1 cup ground eggshells
- 1 cup lard
- 1 cup peanut butter
- 2 cups quick oats
- 2 cups cornmeal
- 1 cup wheat germ
- 1 cup raisins
- sugar (just enough to thicken)

Grind eggshells in a food processor. ● Melt lard over medium heat in medium saucepan and add in ground eggshells. Stir, and continue cooking until eggshells are slightly brown. ● Remove from heat and add peanut butter. Blend in oats, cornmeal, wheat germ, and raisins. Then add some sugar gradually to thicken. Let mixture cool. ● Pour the contents into empty plastic containers, then chill in the freezer until solid. ● Remove from containers and serve in a suet or tray feeder. Store any extra in the freezer in plastic containers or wrap in waxed paper.

Yields: 9 cups or 3 suet molds
Attracts: Bluebirds, Carolina wrens, chickadees, nuthatches, starlings, titmice, and woodpeckers

A deliciously crumby idea

Collect the crumbs from the bottom of cereal boxes before throwing them out. Once you collect a cupful, add it to your favorite suet recipe.

A few grains of wisdom

Salt is very bad for birds, so stick to natural unsalted seeds, nuts, dried fruit, and finely chopped bacon rind.

Heavy Helpings

This fatty treat is a great source of nourishment during the winter months.

- ⅔ cup bacon grease
- 1 cup birdseed or homemade seed mix
- ¼ cup cornmeal
- ½ cup peanut hearts

Melt bacon grease in a heavy pan over medium heat. ● Pour into a medium bowl and add in the birdseed, cornmeal, and peanut hearts, stirring well after each ingredient is added. ● Then pour the mixture into a freezer-safe container and chill in the freezer until hardened. ● Cut portions as needed, serving in a suet feeder or on a tray feeder.

Yields: 2–3 cups

Attracts: A variety of birds, especially bluebirds, Carolina wrens, crows, ravens, starlings, woodpeckers

High-Energy Double-Nut Snack

Birds will flip over the dry dog food in this recipe, which will yield enough to last a few months.

- 5 to 7 pounds of raw suet
- 1 pound fatty bacon
- 2 cups raw peanuts, chopped
- 2 cups raisins
- 1 cup cornmeal
- 2 cups oats
- 1 cup peanut butter
- 1 cup dry dog food, crushed
- 1 cup sunflower hearts
- ½ cup sugar
- ½ cup cracked corn

Cook suet over stove in a large pot (if you do not have a pot big enough, do this in several smaller pots and transfer into a large bowl or other large container) until melted and fry bacon until crisp (save the fat). • Add crumbled bacon and fat to the melted suet, then stir in the nuts, raisins, cornmeal, oats, peanut butter, dog food, sunflower, sugar, and corn. • Allow the mixture to cool completely on a baking sheet and cut into squares that fit your suet feeder, saving any extra in the freezer.

Yields: 8–10 pounds
Attracts: General birds

Doggone yummy

Moistened dog kibble is a favorite treat for many birds that enjoy soft foods. It's especially welcome in winter, when soft food is scarce. Serve some in a wide tray and place on the ground, and in no time you'll see a bevy of thrashers, thrushes, Carolina wrens, mockingbirds, and more.

A little birdie told me . . .

Ground-feeding birds like suet, too, and if it's chopped up, it could mimic grubs. So don't forget to put some in your tray feeders now and again.

Large-Batch Log

If you enjoy providing hearty suet in your feeders but don't have time to make it often, you can prepare in bulk using this recipe and freeze the leftovers for later on.

- 10 pounds yellow cornmeal
- 5 pounds flour
- 7 cups lard
- 3 cups peanut butter
- 10 crushed eggshells
- 3 cups raisins
- 3 cups cracked peanuts

Mix cornmeal with flour in a large container and set aside. • In a large saucepan, melt lard and peanut butter on low heat. When melted, pour the mixture over the combined cornmeal and flour ingredients, blending until it reaches a firm consistency. • Crush the eggshells into a fine powder using a rolling pin, and add them to the mixture. • Also add the raisins and cracked peanuts and stir together. • Roll the mix into a log shape or press into a pan. • Place in the freezer until it's firm enough to cut to fit your suet or tray feeder. • Freeze the extras.

Yields: 15 pounds

Attracts: Bluebirds, Carolina wrens, catbirds, chickadees, mockingbirds, nuthatches, robins, starlings, titmice, woodpeckers

Leftovers Suet

Rely on leftovers and an empty milk carton to create an enjoyable meal for the birds. Woodpeckers especially love this recipe.

Soup grease, leftover trimmed fat from pork chops, beefsteaks, roast chicken, etc.
½ cup black-oil sunflower seeds
2 -qt. cardboard milk carton

Toss your choice of leftovers into a slow cooker and leave overnight on low heat. • In the morning, add the sunflower seeds and pour the mixture into the milk carton. • Once it cools and hardens, slice the carton to the size of your suet feeder, peel the cardboard away, and serve. • Save the leftover slices in a freezer bag or crumble and serve on a tray feeder.

Yields: 1 suet mold
Attracts: General birds

Frozen dinners

Any unused portions of suet can be stored in your freezer for up to two months.

Rendered Suet

Simple suet is made using beef fat, which can be purchased from your neighborhood butcher. Serve it alone, or mix it with berries, mealworms, dried meat, or peanut butter.

1 pound beef fat

First, freeze the fat for at least an hour so it is easier to cut. Using a large knife, cut the fat into strips. • Cook the fat on medium heat in a medium saucepan. Make sure that the fat does not splatter or smoke. When the bottom of the pan is covered in liquid, remove from heat. • Make sure there is a medium bowl set up with a strainer over it. Tip the pan into the strainer, catching the liquid in the bowl. • Take the partially cooked fat from the strainer and return it to the pan and heat again over the stove. Repeat this process once more, or until all the liquid is in the bowl. • This liquid is the rendered fat, which you can now pour into muffin or other baking trays. • Leave in the freezer until it is cold and hard and serve in suet feeders or mesh bags.

Yields: 5 small suet cakes
Attracts: General birds

A suet parfait

Collect leftover cooking grease in coffee cans and store in the freezer. Before adding each layer of grease, throw on a layer of cranberries, nuts, or other delights. In no time you'll have a suet parfait.

No melt? No sweat!

If the temperature goes above 70°F (21°C), suet can melt and turn rancid. Be sure to use a no-melt recipe, which has a doughy texture, in the warmer months (see "No Sweat Suet," page 53) or purchase suet cakes from the store that say "no melt" on the package.

Piecrust Suet

Replace a traditional suet recipe with this yummy piecrust concoction to give the birds variety and keep them interested in your feeders.

1 cup flour
½ cup shortening
¼ tsp. salt
water

Mix all ingredients together in a medium bowl and add enough warm water to mold the contents into a solid ball with your hands. ● This recipe can be served right away without baking and can sit on a suet or tray feeder.

Yields: 1 palm-size molded ball
Attracts: General birds

No-Sweat Suet

Suet can melt and spoil quickly during the summer, but this no-melt suet recipe lets you provide suet all year long.

2 cups quick-cooking oats	½ cup sugar
2 cups cornmeal	1 cup lard
1 cup flour	1 cup crunchy peanut butter

Combine the oats, cornmeal, flour, and sugar in a large bowl. ● Melt the lard and peanut butter and add to the prepared dry ingredients. Mix well. ● Pour into a square pan about 2 inches deep and cut when congealed and put in a suet feeder, or get creative and spread the mix onto tree limbs before it solidifies completely.

Yields: 6 cups

Attracts: General birds, especially bluebirds, Carolina wrens, chickadees, nuthatches, starlings, titmice, and woodpeckers

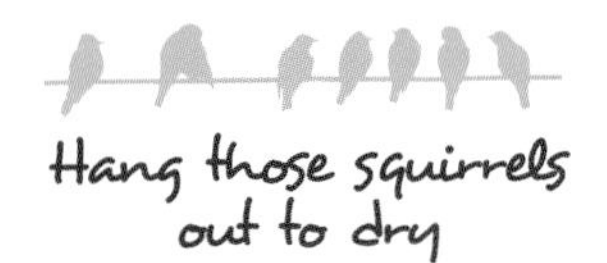

Hang those squirrels out to dry

To deter squirrels, hang a feeder from a clothesline, then cut a hole into the bottom of 2-liter soda bottles and thread them through the clothesline so that they rest on either side of the feeder. The bottles will spin if the squirrels try to run across them! (For more ways to outsmart unwanted visitors, see pages 38 and 39.)

Ultimate Protein Suet

This protein-packed fruit-enhanced suet provides the nutrients birds need throughout their busy day.

- 2 cups lard
- ½ cup chopped orange slices
- ½ cup raisins
- 1 cup wild birdseed or homemade seed mix
- ½ cup peanuts
- 2 cans of tuna or substitute 1 cup of cat food

Melt the lard in a small to medium saucepan on low heat. ● When melted, transfer to a medium-sized bowl and blend in the fruit, seed, and peanuts. Add in either the tuna or cat food. ● To serve, either roll the mix into balls and hang in mesh bags (like the kind used for onions and potatoes), or shape the treat to fit your suet feeder. Store extra in the freezer.

Yields: 8–10 small balls or 2 suet molds
Attracts: Bluebirds, catbirds, chickadees, mockingbirds, nuthatches, orioles, tanagers, thrashers, waxwings, and woodpeckers

Squirrel-Beater Suet

1 pound super-crunchy peanut butter
1 pound lard
⅛ cup cayenne pepper hot sauce
¼ cup dried red pepper flakes
4½ cups cornmeal
4½ cups flour
4 cups rolled oats

Heat the peanut butter and the lard in a large pot over medium heat, stirring occasionally until it melts. • Remove from heat and add the red pepper and hot sauce. • Slowly stir in the flour and cornmeal. When combined, add in the oats and continue to mix everything together. • Scoop mixture into loaf pans and chill until solid. Remove from pan and cut into slices. • Serve outside in mesh bags or suet feeders. • Extras can be stored in your freezer for later use.

Yields: 6 slices
Attracts: Bluebirds, kinglets, nuthatches, pine warblers, woodpeckers, and wrens

A hot vitamin boost

The hot peppers or hot sauce added to recipes to deter squirrels actually provides birds with some extra vitamin C.

Suet and ground-feeding stations are enormously appealing to birds, and each entice a different variety of species, yet both are simple to use and offer birds an array of delicacies.

Suet Feeders

- Suet is a favorite meal for insect eaters such as bluebirds, cardinals, catbirds, chickadees, finches, flickers, mockingbirds, nuthatches, thrashers, titmice, woodpeckers, warblers, and wrens. Once they find this feeder, it will be one of the busiest dining spots in your yard.

- Although the busiest time at your suet feeder will be in the winter, when insects are nearly impossible to find and birds need the high-calorie fat to keep them warm, it's great to keep a suet feeder in your yard all year round. Parent birds will appreciate the feeder in the spring because suet is a perfect soft food to feed their fledglings.

- Suet, or raw beef fat, is usually kept in suet feeders that are in the form of metal wire baskets hung from poles or trees. Store-bought suet blocks and homemade suet recipes are crafted with square suet cages in mind, so you'll notice that many recipes suggest cutting your homemade suet into slices so that it can fit into the feeder. The metal cage is ideal for birds because suet can sometimes be greasy or messy, and the design of this feeder gives the birds as much exposure to the suet as possible without it getting onto the birds feathers, and there's hardly any hassle to fill the feeder.

- Suet is a favorite among squirrels, racoons, and other animals, so unless you animal-proof your feeders, you may find that your suet needs to be resupplied often. Adding some red pepper to your suet mixtures will help (see "Squirrel-Beater Suet," page 55), or try hanging the suet from a pole with a baffle underneath.

Ground Feeders

Ground-feeding birds, such as mourning doves, native sparrows, juncos, and towhees, are the easiest to feed, because all you have to do is scatter seed, bread, or other goodies in your yard and they'll come in droves. They also find food under high feeders, where there is a lot of seed that has spilled over onto the ground. However, seed and other food can quickly turn moldy in wet weather and could thus be harmful to your feathered friends.

To avoid this problem, place a ground feeder in your yard. These feeders are similar in shape to tray or platform feeders, except that they sit on or near the ground. Anything that sits about a foot above the ground is considered a ground feeder. It's important that the bottom of the feeder be a screen or else perforated so that the seed can air dry after rain or snow. As well, the feeder should be placed within 5 or 6 feet of a tree or bush so that the birds can quickly run for cover if they spot a predator nearby. These are easy to make, as all they require are four legs and a screened bottom, but a roof is a great enhancement to help keep out the elements.

Recycle Ideas. . .

There's no need to rush out and purchase a commercial suet feeder. There are so many ways to provide this fatty treat using items you have at home. Or you can just smear the suet directly onto trees!

Mesh Bags

Save the mesh bags that onions or potatoes come in and wrap up the recipes you make, tying the top in a knot. These can be hung from tree branches, but be aware that squirrels also enjoy suet if they can get at it.

Margarine tubs and other containers

Pour suet into yogurt cups, margarine tubs, cat food cans, or other containers that you would normally set out for recycling. Simply pierce a hole in the container and thread some string through, fill with suet, and hang from a tree or a nail. And don't forget to save the containers from any store-bought suet cakes. These are perfectly sized for your metal feeders. Just pour in your mixture from any of the recipes in the Seeds and Suets section, chill in the refrigerator, and you have an instant suet block.

Peanut Butter and Suet in Logs

Search around for a log, drill some holes in it, and place an eye hook at the top for hanging. Smear peanut butter or a suet mixture into the holes and watch the birds enjoy. Another trick is to smear suet or peanut butter into the bark of trees or into the corners of your birdhouses or other birdfeeders.

Fruits and Veggies

Coconuts, dried gourds, and fruit halves make exceptional suet holders! (See "Coconut Concoction," page 71.) You can buy gourds that are pre-dried or dry your own by leaving them outside on the vine until they are dry or by leaving them in a well-ventilated room. Gourds are dry when they become lightweight and the seeds rattle around when you shake it.

To make a feeder, simply trace a large circle onto the face of the gourd and use a jigsaw to cut it out. Scrape out the seeds, drill some holes in the bottom for drainage, and place some wire mesh in the bottom to elevate the birdseed so it doesn't rot. Drill two holes in the top of the gourd and thread some wire through for hanging.

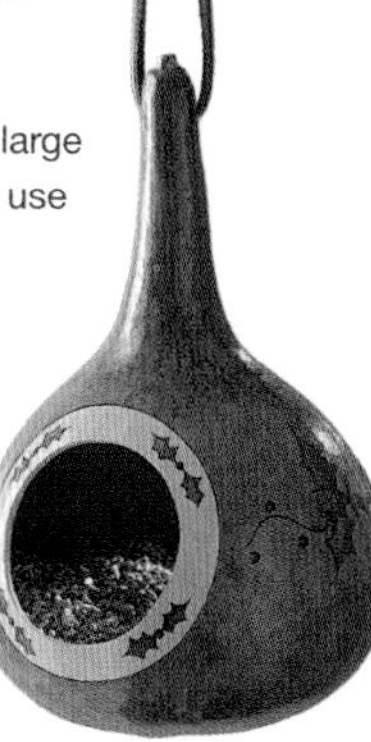

fruity favorites

Offering fruit is one of the best ways to attract a large variety of birds, and it will often bring many species to your backyard that wouldn't ordinarily come otherwise. String some apple slices and cranberries, knead raisins into suet balls, put out a tropical bird buffet of coconut, papaya, and kiwi, or surprise your guests with fruitcakes.

To lure hummingbirds and orioles to your backyard, try whipping up some nectar: Simply mix one part sugar to four parts' boiling water, cool, and pour into your water feeder. This mixture resembles the same sweet taste of the nectar these fruit eaters extract from plants. Here are some quick-and-easy variations on this simple recipe, along with some creative ways to entice the fruit-eaters to your other feeders.

fruity favorites . . .

Basic Bird Nectar

Sweet-toothed birds, like hummingbirds and orioles, love simple and delicious sugary concoctions.

4 cups water
1 cup sugar

Over medium-high heat, bring the water to a boil in a small pot. • Add in the sugar and stir until it dissolves completely. • Remove from heat and let the liquid cool before serving in a water feeder.

Yields: 4 cups
Attracts: Hummingbirds and orioles

CAUTION: Be sure to replace sugar-water mixes every two or three days, especially in warm weather, because they can spoil and make birds sick.

Button it!

Hummingbirds are attracted to the color red. To lure them to feeders, tie a red ribbon to the top, plant red flowers nearby, or throw some red buttons in the water—because they float, you will easily be able to see when your feeder needs a refill!

A little birdie told me . . .

Offer your feathered friends some variety by adding a few drops of vanilla extract to the sugar water.

Citrus Nectar

Warblers, hummingbirds, and orioles will be attracted to this sweet variation on the Basic Bird Nectar.

4 cups water
1 cup sugar
2–3 drops orange extract

Prepare the basic sugar-water mix by boiling the 4 cups of water in a small pot on medium heat and adding the sugar, stirring often so that it dissolves. • Remove from heat and add a few drops of the orange extract. • When cooled, serve in a water feeder.

Yields: 4 cups
Attracts: Hummingbirds, orioles, warblers

A little birdie told me . . .

Fruit flies are a favorite protein-rich snack for hummingbirds and orioles. Hang a banana peel next to your sugar-water feeders and they will happily feast on the fruit flies that stick to the peel.

Bee aware!

Sweet nectar is a favorite among wasps and bees as well as other insects. Purchase a feeder that comes with a bee guard (see yellow insert in photo, opposite). Nevertheless, it has been found that wasps and bees are attracted to the color yellow, so if you find that they are still haunting your feeders, paint the bee guard red.

A little birdie told me . . .

Male hummingbirds don't like to share, so if possible, offer several sugar-water feeders out of sight from one another.

Sweet Oriole Nectar

Oranges and sugar water are sure bets for attracting hummingbirds and orioles, but if you want to offer them something extra special, try grape jelly.

- ⅓ quart grape jelly
- 3 cups water

Mix the jelly in with the water, stirring vigorously (make sure it is mostly dissolved), and serve in a water feeder.

Yields: 4 cups
Attracts: Hummingbirds, orioles

If the ants come marching in . . .

If ants seem to make their way to your hummingbird feeder, coat a section of the pole or the hanger with petroleum jelly to act as a barrier. Be sure to recoat each week.

Mockingbird Muffins

Mockingbirds aren't the only ones who will enjoy these baked goods; the raisins are sure to draw the fruit eaters—woodpeckers, catbirds, and mockingbirds—as well.

1 cup cornmeal	¾ cup currants or raisins
1 cup flour	½ cup bacon drippings
1 cup grated breadcrumbs	¼ tsp. sand
½ tbsp. baking soda	1 cup water

Combine cornmeal, flour, breadcrumbs, and baking soda in a medium to large bowl and blend together with your hands. • Add currants or raisins, bacon drippings, sand, and water. Mix well. • Spoon the moist mixture into a muffin tray lined with paper muffin cups. • Bake at 350°F (177°C) for 15 minutes. Serve these muffins on a tray feeder or spear them onto tree branches.

Yields: 12 muffins

Attracts: A variety of birds, especially bluebirds, Carolina wrens, catbirds, mockingbirds, robins, and woodpeckers

A sweet winter treat

Be sure to serve fruit to your backyard guests from the middle of fall through the winter, when fruit is scarce in the wild.

Berry Bundt Cake

Your feathered friends will surely think it's a celebration when they gather around to feast on this fruit-filled cake.

- 3 cups rendered suet
- 1½ cups chunky peanut butter
- 1 cup mixed dried berries, such as cherries, blueberries, strawberries, and cranberries
- 1 cup sunflower seed hearts
- 1 cup dry oats
- ½ cup corn muffin mix

In a saucepan over low heat, melt the rendered suet and add the chunky peanut butter. • Once the peanut butter is melted, mix in the dried berries and sunflower seed hearts. Then stir in the oatmeal and corn muffin mix. • After all of the ingredients are thoroughly mixed, put the mixture into a jelly mold or Bundt pan and set aside to cool. • To serve whole, place on a tray feeder or slice to the size of your suet feeders.

Yields: 1 cake
Attracts: General birds, especially bluebirds, robins, thrushes, and waxwings

Citrus Surprise

This tangy protein delight will quickly attract birds—and butterflies—to your backyard.

4 hollowed-out lime halves
1 cup peanut butter
1 cup wild birdseed or homemade seed mix

Mix together seed and peanut butter evenly in a small bowl, then spoon the mixture into hollowed-out lime halves. • Serve these on a tray feeder.

Yields: 4 seed-filled lime halves

Attracts: Bluebirds, cardinals, Carolina wrens, chickadees, mockingbirds, nuthatches, orioles, robins, starlings, titmice, and woodpeckers

A little birdie told me...

You don't need to be limited to fresh and dried fruits—birds love frozen fruit, too! Buy them in season and freeze them in plastic bags for winter feeding.

Simple citrus server

You can also serve your feathered friends by spooning this mixture into hollowed-out grapefruit halves. Use a pencil to pierce the rind in three places, attach a ribbon, and hang from a tree.

Coconut Concoction

For a tropical specialty, treat your feeder birds to a coconut creation.

1 coconut
½ cup bacon grease
2 cups wild birdseed or homemade seed mix

Split the coconut in half and drain the liquid. • Drill three evenly spaced holes around each coconut for hanging. • Mix together the bacon grease and birdseed, wetting as much of the seeds as possible with the fat. • Fill the coconut halves with the bacon-greased seed and serve by hanging on a tree branch with heavy string or thick yarn (do not hang from a feeder unless the feeder is mounted to the ground by a pole).

Yields: 2 coconut halves
Attracts: A variety of birds, especially chickadees, goldfinches, and sparrows

A little birdie told me . . .

Feed birds at the same time every day and they will get to know your routine and greet you as you fill the feeders.

NOTE: To make the coconut feeder opposite, use a jigsaw to cut out a large circle and then remove the insides. Drill holes in the top for hanging and fill feeder with seed or suet mixtures.

Second-story feeders

If the idea of watching birds from your second-floor bedroom window sounds appealing but refilling the feeder has left you in a quandary, here's a simple solution: Attach a small pulley to the soffit of the overhang outside the window, thread some thin nylon rope through it, and attach one end of the rope to a birdfeeder using an S hook. Secure the rope down below by wrapping the end around a cleat attached to the siding or a nearby tree. Now you can hoist the feeder up and down from ground level each time the birds need a fresh meal.

Fruity Tweet Bars

This fruit-and-vegetable blend is so delicious, birds will devour it in a matter of hours.

- 1 cup peanut butter
- 1 cup oats
- 1 cup corn muffin mix
- 1 cup canned corn
- 1 cup raisins
- 1 cup wild birdseed or homemade seed mix
- ⅓ cup chopped apples
- ⅓ cup chopped grapes

In a large bowl, combine all ingredients and work with your hands or a long wooden or metal spoon. The consistency should be thicker than cookie dough. • Mold the paste into squares and then serve in your suet or tray feeder. • If there is some left over, wrap it in plastic and store in the freezer.

Yields: 10 square bars

Attracts: Bluebirds, Carolina wrens, chickadees, mockingbirds, nuthatches, robins, starlings, thrashers, titmice, towhees, and woodpeckers

Raisin Cake

This recipe is a favorite among fruit eaters such as bluebirds, catbirds, and mockingbirds, but you will be pleasantly surprised by the other birds that will eagerly snap up this delightful treat.

- 1 cup cornmeal
- 1 cup uncooked oatmeal
- ½ cup lard
- 1 cup skim milk
- 1 cup wheat germ
- 1 cup flour
- 1 cup raisins

Mix together the cornmeal, oatmeal, lard, wheat germ, and skim milk in a medium to large bowl and blend well to form a thick batter. Then add raisins and flour. • Grease a pie pan and flour lightly for baking. Pour mixture into pie pan and bake at 350°F (177°C) for approximately 1 hour. • Take out of the oven and set aside to cool. • Finally, break the cake into large pieces to hang in mesh bags.

Yields: 5 large broken pieces
Attracts: Bluebirds, orioles, robins, thrushes, and waxwings

Location, location, location

An evergreen is an ideal location for birdfeeders because its thick foliage shields harsh wind and offers a year-round hiding place from predators.

Baked Bird Pie

The red pepper in this hearty pie will go unnoticed by birds but is sure to keep the squirrels at bay.

- 2 cups cornmeal
- 6 cups water
- ½ cup bacon drippings
- 1 cup flour
- 1 tbsp. sand
- 1 cup molasses
- ½ tsp. baking powder
- 1 tsp. red pepper
- 1 cup any kind of nuts
- ½ cup raisins
- additional water as necessary

Boil water in a large pot on medium-high heat. Add the cornmeal and allow to bubble for a few minutes. • Remove from heat and let cool. • Add the remaining ingredients: bacon drippings, flour, sand, molasses, baking powder, red pepper, nuts, and raisins. If necessary, add additional water to bind the mixture together. • Pack into small foil pie pans. • Bake in the oven at 400°F (204°C) until brown and hang serve in a tray feeder or hange foil pans from backyard trees using heavy string or yarn.

Yields: 4–5 small pies

Attracts: Bluebirds, Carolina wrens, crows, ravens, starlings, and woodpeckers

A little birdie told me . . .

Adding a little bit of sand to bird food helps aid their digestion.

A little birdie told me...

If you have a large yard, a mulberry tree is the best fruit-bearing tree you can plant to attract birds. For smaller yards a cherry tree is ideal.

Tropical Treat

This coconut suet is guaranteed to bring a flurry of birds to your feeder.

- 1 cup lard
- 1 cup peanut butter
- ⅓ cup coconut
- 2 cups oats
- 2 cups cornmeal
- ¼ cup raisins
- ¼ cup wild birdseed or homemade seed mix

Melt the lard and peanut butter in a medium saucepan on low heat. • Stir in coconut, oats, and cornmeal. • Add the raisins and birdseed and pour it all into a deep medium-sized baking pan and leave it to chill in the refrigerator overnight to solidify. • The next day, remove from the refrigerator and cut into squares to serve in a suet or tray feeder. • Wrap extra in plastic and freeze.

Yields: 10 squares

Attracts: Bluebirds, catbirds, chickadees, mockingbirds, nuthatches, orioles, tanagers, thrashers, waxwings, and woodpeckers

Hummingbird Feeders . . .

Although the name suggests that only hummingbirds use this type of feeder, it is also a favorite for orioles, tanagers, and catbirds as well.

- Hummingbird feeders provide the sugar-rich liquid that is similar to the sweet nectar that hummingbirds and orioles gain from plants such as salvia, foxglove, and verbena. The basic nectar recipe is four parts water to one part sugar, but there are several variations on this recipe (see pages 63–66), with citrus flavors and jellies being the most frequent flavors added, causing these birds to hover around these sweet feeders for long visits daily.

- There are two common types of hummingbird feeders, one being a tube, shaped like the tube seed feeder, which includes an extra tailpiece used to hold and release liquid in the presence of a feeding bird. The second feeder design is more like a bowl, held midair by a pole. This saucer-style feeder is great when held in the hands to attract birds directly to you, but otherwise it can dry out or become visited more often by bees or wasps.

It is necessary to refill a hummingbird feeder often, not only because each tiny hummingbird can drink up to half a cup of sugar water every day but because the sugar water can spoil after a few days, especially in the warmer months.

The color yellow

It's been said that the color yellow attracts bees and wasps, so it's best to choose a hummingbird feeder that doesn't display this color. If yours does, simply paint the yellow parts red.

Providing water for backyard visitors . . .

Birds—especially chickadees, goldfinches, grackles, robins, and sparrows—love to splash around in water. In fact, to some it's as alluring as a fully stocked feeder. Birds use water to remove dust and parasites from their feathers, to quench their thirst, and to simply have fun.

Birdbaths

Adding at least one water source to your backyard will quickly attract a number of birds. Birdbaths, of course, are the first source that usually comes to mind. Although garden centers and online sites offer a plethora of elaborate birdbaths, birds don't really care what they bathe in. They'll use anything from a terra-cotta plant saucer to a frying pan, as long as the water is fresh, free of algae, and isn't too deep. They prefer water that is only 1 to 3 inches deep; if your basin is deeper, add some flat rocks to the bottom.

The classic birdbath is one that is usually presented on a pedestal about waist high, but there are also ones that attach to a deck, dishes that can be placed at ground level or on a stump, rock wall, or table, and even heated birdbaths! These are great in colder climates. You can either purchase a heating unit for an existing birdbath, or purchase a heated model.

Where you display the birdbath is critical, too, for viewing and for safety. It's important to display birdbaths near bushes or some other feature that birds can utilize if danger approaches. Cats are drawn to birds splashing around in birdbaths, so if you have a cat, it would be better to display a hanging birdbath. The bottom of the basin should be rough so birds can secure a proper footing, and a dark-color basin will attract their attention.

Of all the different ways to provide water, though, standing water is actually the least tempting presentation for birds because it will take them a while to notice it. They are more attracted to the sound of running water. A simple solution is to add a motion accessory to the birdbath. A hose dripping into a pond is very effective, as is running the lawn sprinkler for a few hours.

Misters are highly effective in the warmer months, and hummingbirds love to hover in them.

They can be attached to your garden hose or drip right into your birdbath. The ideal spot to position a mister is in a shaded area where there are several natural perches for birds to rest on.

A pond, especially with a waterfall or fountain, is also ideal. Make sure there are shallow places where birds can splash around and several places for them to perch and have a drink.

Dustbaths

Believe it or not, a dustbath is just as refreshing for birds that are trying to cool down in the warm weather. Dustbaths help to soak up any moisture and oil and helps to remove parasites. If you have a patch of soil in your backyard, you may find birds frolicking in it, loosening up the soil, and even rolling in it. If you don't have a natural source, you can make one very easily by finding a sunny spot in your yard, cutting out a patch of grass about 3 feet square, and digging down about 6 inches. Fill the area with equal parts of sand and leaf loam or peat moss. Finally, line the area with bricks or rocks.

Ping-Pong balls

Floating a Ping-Pong ball in a birdbath during the winter will help prevent ice from forming.

Plants and the Birds They Attract . . .

Plants with Berries	Birds They Attract
Arrowwood *Viburnum dentatum*	Cardinals, flycatchers, grouse, robins, starlings, thrashers, thrushes, waxwings, woodpeckers
Elderberries *Sambucus*	Blackbirds, bluebirds, buntings, cardinals, catbirds, flickers, grosbeaks, grouse, jays, kinglets, magpies, mockingbirds, nuthatches, orioles, pigeons, robins, sapsuckers, sparrows, starlings, tanagers, thrushes, titmice, towhees, vireos, waxwings, woodpeckers, wrens
Serviceberry *Amelanchier laevis*	Bluebirds, cardinals, jays, robins, thrashers, waxwings, woodpeckers
Strawberries *Fragaria and hybrids*	Catbirds, crows, grosbeaks, grouse, mockingbirds, thrushes, towhees
Sumac *Rhus*	Bluebirds, bobwhites, cardinals, catbirds, crows, finches, flickers, grosbeaks, grouse, jays, junco, magpies, mockingbirds, pigeons, starlings, tanagers, thrashers, thrushes, vireos, warblers, woodpeckers, wrens

Shrubs/ Grasses	Birds They Attract
Beauty Bush *Kolkwitzia amabilis*	Cardinals, mockingbirds, robins, thrashers, woodpeckers
Big Bluestem *Andropogon gerardii*	Blackbirds, meadowlarks, sparrows
Flowering Dogwood *Cornus*	Bluebirds, cardinals, flickers, grosbeaks, mockingbirds, robins, tanagers, thrushes, woodpeckers
Holly *Ilex*	Catbirds, crows, grosbeaks, grouse, mockingbirds, thrushes, towhees
Indian Grass *Sorghastrum nutans*	Juncos, sparrows

Annuals	Birds They Attract
Cosmos *Cosmos*	Buntings, finches, juncos, sparrows
Garden Balsam *Impatiens balsamina*	Cardinals, grosbeaks, hummingbirds, sparrows
Mexican Sunflower *Tithonia rotundifolia*	Buntings, cardinals, chickadees, finches, hummingbirds, jays, nuthatches
Tickseed Sunflower *Bidens aristosa*	Buntings, chickadees, finches, sparrows, titmice
Zinnias *Zinnia*	Buntings, chickadees, finches, sparrows, titmice

Perennials	Birds They Attract
Anise Hyssop *Agastache foeniculum*	Finches, hummingbirds, sparrows
Coneflower *Echinacea purpurea*	Finches
Goldenrod *Solidago*	Buntings, chickadees, sparrows, titmice
Mulleins *Verbascum thapsus*	Bluebirds, chickadees, finches, titmice, warblers, woodpeckers
Yellow Giant Hyssop *Agastache nepetoides*	Buntings, chickadees, hummingbirds, sparrows, titmice, warblers, woodpeckers

If you come across a baby bird . . .

Don't react by picking it up right away, thinking it is abandoned. Many times this isn't the case. If you're uncertain, contact your local animal shelter or wildlife bird rehabilitation center.

Songbird fledglings—fuzzy little birds that can hop about but aren't yet adept at flying—often hide in groundcover for days after they make that first leap out of the nest. This is a vulnerable time for them; they are similar to toddlers in that they are learning new skills but still need their parents' help. Don't intervene. Their parents are close by, and they do check often to see how their fledglings are doing. Once these young birds are ready, they will fly away.

Baby birds sometimes fall out of their nests, but this is unusual unless there has been a storm or other natural disaster. If you see a featherless baby bird on the ground and you spot a nest just above, it's better to place him back in the nest to keep him safe from predators, like house cats. Birds have a poor sense of smell, so you don't have to worry about the mother abandoning the nest if it smells your scent. If you can't find the nest, make one out of a small berry container or basket and be sure that there are holes in the bottom so that it can't hold water. Place some dry leaves and grass in it and wire it to a branch about 5 feet off the ground in a tree close to where you found the bird. Then place the nestling in it. If you keep your distance, the parents will find the nestling.

If for some reason you do come across an injured bird or an abandoned nestling, contact a wildlife rehabilitator (you can go online or contact your local animal shelter or wildlife bird rehabilitation center). Before intervening, though, it is essential to be sure that this is the case. If the bird is limping or dragging its wing, it's obviously hurt. You must not try to pick up the bird unless advised by the rehabilitator to do so. Moreover, you must not try to feed the bird. You will probably end up doing more harm than good.

The one thing you can do, though, is provide shelter for the bird so it is comfortable while you wait for the wildlife rehabilitator. Sometimes they

Fledgling or nestling?

If you're not sure whether the bird is a fledgling or a nestling, allow the bird to perch on your finger. If the bird can grip it, it's a fledgling.

may even ask you to transport it to the center. If so, construct an improvised nest in your home using an old shoebox, and line the inside with lots of cotton, soft linen, or toilet paper to keep the bird warm and comfortable. You could heat the bottom using a heating pad, but place only half the box on it so the bird can move away from the heat if it gets too warm. You could also place hot-water bottles around the edges of the shoebox or warm a towel in the microwave for two minutes and place it inside the box. Move the bird to a dark, quiet place away from pets and children.

Recycle Ideas and Hummingbird Feeder Project . . .

Here are some great ways to turn household items into wonderful feeders, birdseed catchers, birdbaths, or shelter for the birds!

Household items

- Use a cover from an old garbage can or spaghetti pot for a birdbath.
- Suspend a three-tiered hanging wire fruit basket and fill it with suet treats.
- Prop up an old window screen to create a platform feeder.
- Hang an array of teacups by their handles and stuff them with suet.

Birdseed catcher

If you're trying to avoid a mound of tossed-out seeds and hulls from collecting at the base of your feeder, mount a round plastic sled to the feeder pole. Cut a hole the size of the pole in the middle of the sled, slide it over the pole, and place a hose clamp midway up to keep it stationary. Now you have a two-tiered feeder!

Hummingbird Feeder Project

You'll be amazed at how fun and easy it is to make this one-of-a-kind feeder using a recycled glass bottle. And with the copper accents, it's a decorative addition to your backyard as well. Once a hummingbird discovers your feeder, it will come back again and again.

Materials

Glass bottle
5 feet of 4-gauge untreated copper wire
Hummingbird feeding tube
Beads or other decorations
(Remember, hummingbirds love red!)
D ring or carabiner
Screw eye

Tools

File
Needle-nose pliers
Wire cutter

1. File the ends of the copper wires so there are no sharp edges.
2. Take the 4-gauge wire and bend it at one end to form a small circle. This should fit loosely over the opening of the bottle.
3. Insert the bottle into the circle and make one more loop around the neck to hold it securely.
4. Wind the rest of the wire around the bottle, creating your own design but leaving 18 inches or so of wire so that you can make a large loop for hanging and then a fashion loop at the end to secure it (see image at right). The wire should be loose enough that you can easily remove the bottle for refilling, but tight enough to hold the feeder securely.
5. Next, decorate with the 12-gauge copper wire using the needle-nose pliers and wire cutters as needed. To create the look of curling vines, wrap the wire around a pencil first and attach in pieces.
6. Use colorful beads or other adornments to complete your design.
7. Remove the bottle and fill it with sugar water. Then take your feeding tube and gently twist the stopper into place. It should fit snugly to avoid leaking.
8. Place the bottle back into the copper holder and hang it by hooking the feeder onto a snap ring.

peanut butter pleasures

Peanut butter is high in fat and full of protein, and it is a great means for affixing seed to pinecones, bread, and tree bark. What's more, feeder birds—especially woodpeckers, chickadees, and titmice—love it. But it's not a food you want to offer birds in great quantities, because it's sticky and messy and could get all over their feathers if not offered in a suitable way. Here are some great ways to present your backyard friends with this much-loved fare.

peanut butter pleasures . . .

Bark Bird Meal

Pleasantly surprise woodpeckers by pressing this mixture into the bark of a tree.

- 1 cup shortening
- 1 cup peanut butter
- 1 cup flour
- 4 cups cornmeal

Mix together all the ingredients in a large bowl until it reaches the consistency of putty. ● Outside, use your fingers or a spoon to press the mixture into the bark of trees and the corners of your birdfeeders.

Yields: 8 cups mix
Attracts: Bluebirds, Carolina wrens, chickadees, nuthatches, starlings, titmice, and woodpeckers

Cornmeal creations

Cornmeal is a great staple to have on hand because it can be mixed with binding agents such as peanut butter, canola oil, bacon grease, or sunflower oil to make a simple "doughy" treat for your backyard visitors. Experiment by adding in some special morsels, like currants, raisins, nuts, bacon, apples, or cranberries, or whatever else you find in your pantry or refrigerator. You may come up with a real winner!

Peanut Butter Banana Pudding

This quick-and-easy banana mixture is high in protein and will provide comfort in the winter if served at room temperature or, if chilled, will make a refreshing treat during the summer months.

1 banana
½ cup peanut butter
1 tbsp. wheat germ
¼ cup oatmeal

Mash banana and peanut butter together, then add wheat germ and oatmeal. ● Serve either chilled or at room temperature in yogurt cups or other similar container.

Yields: 1 cup

Attracts: Blackbirds, buntings cardinals, catbirds, chickadees, goldfinches, grosbeaks, juncos, mockingbirds, orioles, sparrows, tanagers, thrashers, titmice, towhees, warblers, woodpeckers, and wrens

Beaky Breakfast

Mixing lard with cereal and other simple ingredients provides a delicious treat that will help keep birds warm in winter.

- 2 quarts water
- 1 cup lard
- 4 cups dry cereal
- 1 cup peanut butter
- 1 tbsp. wheat germ
- ¾ cup sunflower seeds
- 5 pinecones (optional)

Bring water and lard to a boil in a medium pot over medium-high heat. • Add cereal, then turn heat to medium-low and simmer for 15 minutes. • Remove from heat and mix in peanut butter, wheat germ, and sunflower seeds. Let cool in a plastic container and serve on a tray feeder, or you can press the treat into pinecones and hang from a tree.

Yields: 5–6 cups or 5 pinecones

Attracts: Bluebirds, Carolina wrens, chickadees,nuthatches, starlings, titmice, and woodpeckers

A little birdie told me . . .

Birds rely on feeders most during the winter because it is more difficult for them to find natural food sources then.

Bagel bonanza

If you have a leftover bagel, even a stale one, cover it with peanut butter, then roll it in a combination of cornmeal and birdseed. Thread some yarn through the hole and hang it from a tree!

Peanut Butter Supreme

There's something for everyone in this supreme high-energy recipe!

- ½ pound lard or suet
- 2 cups breadcrumbs
- ⅓ cup unsalted nuts, chopped
- 3 apples, chopped
- ⅓ cup raisins (dried cranberries can also be used)
- ½ cup honey
- ¼ cup cornmeal
- ½ cup flour
- 1 cup black-oil sunflower seeds
- ½ cup rolled oats
- 1 cup peanut butter
- muffin cups

Melt the lard or suet on low heat in saucepan. • Mix in the rest of the ingredients. • Spoon mixture into muffin cups or shape into balls and set aside to cool. • Serve in tray feeders or hanging mesh bags (the type onions or potatoes come in). • Wrap extras in plastic wrap and store in freezer until needed.

Yields: 18 muffin cups or balls
Attracts: General birds

Honey Crunch Cake

This is a sweet treat served in mesh bags that will intrigue your backyard birds.

- 1 cup lard
- 1 cup crunchy peanut butter
- ½ cup honey
- 2 eggs (with shells)
- 1 cup oats
- 1 tsp. baking soda
- 2 cups whole wheat flour

Mix all ingredients together in a medium to large bowl and pour into a greased 9-inch square pan. • Bake at 350°F (177°C) for 30–40 minutes or until toothpick inserted in the center comes out clean. • Cool before removing from pan, and hang this treat from trees or birdfeeders using mesh bags (like the ones in which you buy onions, fruit, or potatoes).

Yields: 1 cake

Attracts: Bluebirds, Carolina wrens, chickadees, crows, grackles, juncos, magpies, nuthatches, purple martins, sparrows, starlings, titmice, and woodpeckers

Pinching peanuts

Save pennies by buying generic peanut butter or stretching it by mixing it with cornmeal.

Peanut Butter Puff Balls

These peanut butter treats require no baking, so they can be served right away.

- 1 cup peanut butter
- ½ cup cornmeal
- ¼ cup honey
- ¼ cup raisins
- ¼ cup wild birdseed or homemade seed mix
- 1–2 cups water, or as needed

Combine all ingredients (peanut butter, cornmeal, honey, raisins, birdseed) except water into a large mixing bowl. • Add the water slowly until mixture is workable, then form into 1-inch balls and serve on a tray feeder.

Yields: 10 peanut butter balls

Attracts: General birds, especially bluebirds, Carolina wrens, chickadees, nuthatches, starlings, titmice, and woodpeckers

A little birdie told me . . .

Sprinkling cornmeal, which is high in fat and protein, over snow will attract ground-feeding birds such as doves, juncos, sparrows, and towhees.

Spicy Peanut Seed

Birds love this spicy seed, but squirrels don't!

- 2 cups peanut butter
- 2 cups lard
- ½ cup flour
- ½ cup old-fashioned oats
- ½ cup Spanish peanuts
- ½ cup raisins
- ½ cup sunflower seeds
- ½ cup cracked corn
- 1 tsp. hot pepper

Melt peanut butter and lard together in a medium saucepan on medium heat. • Remove from heat and pour into a large mixing bowl. • Fold in the flour and oats first, then add the peanuts, raisins, sunflower seeds, corn, and pepper. Mix well. • From the bowl, transfer the mix into a large cake pan and refrigerate until hardened. • Cut into pieces and place in a suet feeder.

Yields: 5–6 cups
Attracts: General birds

A little birdie told me . . .

You should never feed birds straight peanut butter, because it can glue their beaks together.

Pastamania

Birds love pasta whether it's cooked or not. Boil up some elbows with peas, carrots, and corn, let cool, and serve in a tray feeder. For an uncooked version, fill dry penne with peanut butter.

Substitute Suet Sandwich

A protein-packed peanut butter sandwich can be exactly what a hungry bird needs for a lunchtime meal.

2 slices of any soft bread
8 tbsp. peanut butter
½ cup wild birdseed or homemade seed mix

Lightly toast the bread slices and spread the peanut butter on all four sides, using about 2 tbsp. peanut butter per side. • Spread birdseed out on a paper plate and press the slices into birdseed to coat the peanut butter. • Put the two slices together like a sandwich and place in a suet feeder for the birds to enjoy.

Yields: 1 sandwich
Attracts: General birds

Sunflower Surprise

Birds are attracted to sunflowers for their seeds, which are ideal for the protein and oil they provide. Treat your backyard friends to a surprise by filling the heads with this wonderful peanut butter treat.

- 5 sunflower heads
- 1 cup water
- 1 cup yellow cornmeal
- ½ cup oats
- ½ cup peanut butter
- 1 ½ cup wild birdseed or homemade seed mix

Boil water on medium-high in a small to medium pot and mix in just enough cornmeal to cook into a soft mixture. • Remove the pot from heat and add oats, peanut butter, and birdseed. Make sure the ingredients do not get too thick. • When the mixture cools, use a spoon to press it into sunflower heads, then hang from a tree or feeder with string.

Yields: Enough mixture to cover 5 sunflower heads

Attracts: Most birds, especially cardinals, chickadees, finches, grosbeaks, nuthatches, titmice, and woodpeckers

A sunflower celebration

Birds can't resist sunflower seeds. Grow a tall hedge of them in your yard and you'll see cardinals, chickadees, finches, nuthatches, and titmice scrambling for the flower head, while ground feeders will search the area below for dropped seeds.

Recycle Project: Juice Bottle Feeder. . .

This homemade feeder made mostly from recycled materials is as attractive as an expensive store-bought model. Use plywood for the roof and feeding tray because it will stand up to the elements, but disguise it a bit with some cedar edging.

Materials

1-gallon plastic juice bottle with cap
Sheet of paper large enough to wrap once around the bottle
Plywood scraps at least ½-inch thick
Cedar scraps
1-¼-inch galvanized deck screws
1-½-inch wire brads
Small sheet-metal screws
18-inch-long light-duty rustproof chain
Two S hooks
Tools
Table saw
Saber saw
Permanent marker
Utility knife or scissors
Compass
Power drill

1 Using the permanent marker, mark the plastic juice bottle at least ¾ inches below the point where the bottle straightens out. Wrap a piece of paper around the bottom of the bottle, lining up the edge of the paper with the point you've marked. Trace around the edge of the paper with the marker to make a cutting line. Carefully cut along the line with the utility knife or scissors. Drill three ½-inch holes in the narrowest part of the bottle's neck. Don't worry too much about the size of the holes. You can enlarge them later if necessary.

2 To make the seed tray, cut a scrap of plywood 6 ½ inches square. Rip trim pieces to make the tray 1-inch deep (thickness of plywood plus 1 inch). They'll overlap at the four corners, so the tray trim pieces should measure 6½ inches plus the thickness of the plywood. Attach them to the tray with the 1-½-inch wire brads and drill a ¼-inch drainage hole in each corner of the seed tray.

3 To make the roof, cut a scrap of plywood 10 inches square. Trim the roof edging in the same manner as the seed tray. From another scrap of plywood, cut a disk to fit the diameter of the wide part of the bottle, using the compass to draw the circle and a saber saw to cut. Center and attach the disk to the underside of the roof with four deck screws.

From the opposite corners of the roof, draw four straight pencil lines. They should meet in the center of the board. (It's important that this hole be centered so that the feeder hangs straight.) Drill a hole through this center point large enough for the chain to thread through.

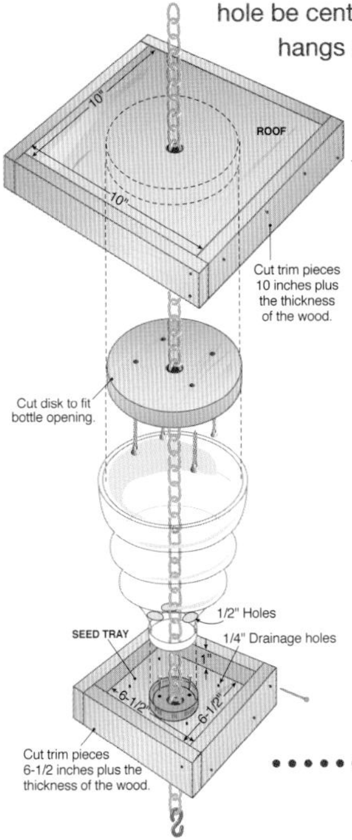

ROOF

10"

10"

Cut trim pieces 10 inches plus the thickness of the wood.

Cut disk to fit bottle opening.

1/2" Holes

SEED TRAY

1/4" Drainage holes

1"

6-1/2"

6-1/2"

Cut trim pieces 6-1/2 inches plus the thickness of the wood.

4 Remove the cap from the bottle and drill two holes near its outside edge. Start with a small drill bit and gradually increase the size until the sheet-metal screws fit through the holes easily. Center the cap upside down in the feeding tray and

attach with the small screws, but don't tighten too much or the cap will crack.

5 Drill a hole through the center of the bottle cap and tray, then string the chain through the roof, bottle, and tray (see inset). Loop the top of the chain or use an S hook for hanging. Attach another S hook at the bottom to keep the chain from slipping through the feeder. Close the hook with pliers, then fill up the feeder with seed and hang it up in your yard so the birds can enjoy.

seasonal treats

Each season brings with it some advantages and disadvantages when it comes to finding food in the wild. Here are some wonderful treats, along with some expert tips, to keep your feathered friends happy and healthy all year long. Yet birds should not be the only ones on the receiving end of these delicious, nutritious treats. Some also make a perfect gift for those bird-loving friends and relatives on your holiday list.

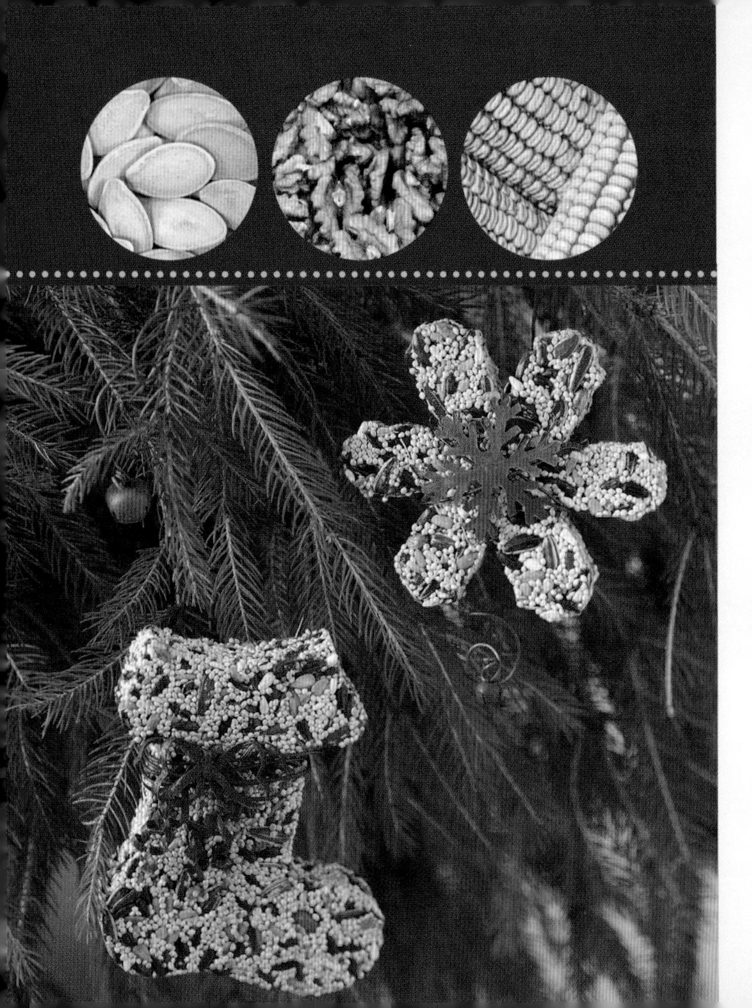

seasonal treats . . .

Tasty Holiday Ornaments

Surprise your feathered friends with a tree decorated with edible ornaments for the holidays.

¾ cup flour
½ cup water
3 tbsp. corn syrup
4 cups birdseed mix
wax paper
toothpick

Mix ingredients together in a bowl. If mixture is too dry, add a little more corn syrup and water as necessary to moisten. • Turn out the mixture on waxed paper and use a rolling pin to flatten. • Cut shapes out of the birdseed mixture with holiday cookie cutters. • Using a toothpick, pierce a hole in the shape for hanging. • Dry them on wax paper for 4–6 hours on each side. • Attach to trees with raffia or ribbon or wrap up in cellophane and offer them to someone on your holiday list.

Yields: Approximately 6 ornaments
Attracts: General birds

Time to string the donuts

Decorate trees outside for the holidays by stringing day-old donuts into a garland.

Holiday tree trimmings

Surprise your feathered friends by hanging miniature stockings stuffed with seed and millet sprigs around your yard.

Bird Baubles

Wrapped up in cellophane and tied with festive ribbon, these healthy treats are the perfect holiday gift for your bird-loving friends.

- 3 cups oats
- 1 quart water
- 1 pound lard
- 1 jar of peanut butter (12 oz.)
- 3 cups cornmeal
- 1 cup uncooked Cream of Wheat

Cook oats in a large pot on medium-high heat in boiling water for 2 minutes. • Remove from heat and stir in lard and peanut butter until melted. • Add cornmeal and Cream of Wheat and stir. • Cool and shape into balls. • Form each ball around a ribbon or string for hanging from trees or feeders.

Yields: 15 baubles

Attracts: Bluebirds, Carolina wrens, chickadees, nuthatches, starlings, titmice, and woodpeckers

An eggcellent source of nutrition

Eggs provide nutrients, and birds love them. Some, such as crows, grackles, jays, and ravens, will even steal eggs from other nests for their valuable insides. So next time you have some leftover scrambled eggs, serve them to your feathered friends; they'll happily gobble them up!

Bird Bells

These simple bell-shaped treats can be molded using an empty plastic container from your recycling bin.

2 eggs
2 tbsp. honey
wild birdseed or homemade seed mix,
  as much as necessary to fill the container
1 small, empty plastic container
  (such as a cup, used margarine tub, or yogurt cup)

In a medium bowl, blend the eggs and honey with a fork, adding birdseed until the mixture holds its shape. • Using a skewer, poke a small hole through the bottom of the container. • Pull a loop of yarn or string through the hole, leaving about 2 inches outside the container and 2 or more inches inside the container. • Fill the container with the seed mixture and let set for about 5 days until completely solid. • Remove the hardened seed from the plastic container and hang the treat from a tree branch.

Yields: 1 bell mold
Attracts: Chickadees, crows, grackles, juncos, magpies, purple martins, ravens, sparrows, and starlings

Summer Heat Bird Treat

This recipe is best served in weather above 70°F (21°C).

1 cup water
1 cup oats
¾ cup bacon grease or substitute melted lard
1 cup uncooked Cream of Wheat
1 cup cornmeal
½ cup raisins
1 cup creamy peanut butter
2 handfuls wild birdseed or homemade seed mix

Boil water in a medium pot on medium-high heat and add oats. • Reduce heat to low and simmer for 1 minute. • Remove pot from stove and immediately add in bacon grease, Cream of Wheat, cornmeal, raisins, peanut butter, and bird seed. • Stir together well. • Let the mixture cool, and place in suet feeder for immediate use. • Freeze unused portions in resealable bags.

Yields: 5 cups
Attracts: General birds

A little birdie told me . . .

Most birds visit suet feeders in winter, but it's important to have a suet feeder in summer because this soft food is excellent for nestlings and hatchlings.

A little birdie told me . . .

Fledglings love cottage cheese. Mix in some raisins, blueberries, or sliced grapes for added flavor and set out in shallow containers. Remember to take this special treat back inside after a few hours or else the cheese will spoil.

Bread for the Babies

In summer, fledglings need to be introduced to new foods, which should be soft and mild tasting. Here's an easy recipe that's perfect for baby birds.

3 tsp. sugar
2 cups milk
2 slices white bread

Cut bread into small squares and set aside. • Mix sugar and milk together in a bowl. • Soak bread in milk mixture for a few seconds and place pieces in tray feeder.

Yields: 2 slices of bread

Edible Summer Arrangement

Delight fruit eaters with a "fruit tree" made by spearing an assortment of colorful fruit onto nails hammered halfway into a wooden post.
Suggested fruits:

- Quartered oranges
- Chunks of banana
- Large pieces of apple
- Whole cherries
- Seasonal berries
- Chunks of cantaloupe
- Chunks of pineapple

Attracts: Bluebirds, buntings, cardinals, catbirds, finches, grosbeaks, mockingbirds, orioles, tanagers, warblers, waxwings, and woodpeckers

A little birdie told me . . .

Spring and summer are the most challenging times for wild birds. During this period they scout out their territory, go through spring molting, mate and build nests, and welcome their babies into the world. So it's important to make sure feeders are stock full of high-energy foods.

A little birdie told me...

Never throw away bruised or mushy apples. Chop them up and place them in tray feeders or simply toss the apple pieces onto the ground. Birds will even scramble for the cores.

Autumn Harvest Mix

The dried apples in this autumn-inspired treat will delight hungry feeder birds and stay fresh and edible well into the season.

- 2 cups chopped apples, dried
- 2 cups raisins
- 2 cups chopped walnuts
- 1 cup chopped prunes
- 1 cup dried squash seeds
- 1 cup pumpkin seeds

Combine all ingredients in a large bowl and mix. • Then fill your tray or seed feeders with this autumn snack. • Pour any extra into a paper or plastic bag and store in a cool and dry place.

Yields: 9 cups

Attracts: Bluebirds, Carolina wrens, chickadees, mockingbirds, robins, starlings, thrashers, titmice, and towhees

Trick or Tweet

Surprise ground-feeding birds in the fall by filling a hollowed-out pumpkin with cracked corn and mixed birdseed.

1 small pumpkin
2 cups wild birdseed or homemade seed mix
2 cups cracked corn

Hollow out the pumpkin, removing both the seeds and innards, creating a "bowl." • Fill it with cracked corn and seed for an autumn treat. • You can leave it on the ground under a bird feeder or place it on a tray feeder.

Yields: 1 pumpkin or 4 cups
Attracts: Ground feeders, especially cardinals, doves, goldfinches, juncos, sparrows, and towhees.

Stock up and save

In the fall many garden centers discount their seed, so it's a great time to stock up. Seed can last for months if stored properly in airtight containers.

Feeding Tips for Every Season . . .

Winter, spring, summer, fall—when it comes to birds, you're always on call. Bird feeding is a year-round commitment, and birds' needs change along with the change in weather. Here are a few strategies to keep your feathered friends happy and well fed all year long.

Winter

This is the time when birds depend on your generosity the most. Cold weather has diminished the insects, wild berries, and natural seed normally gracing your yard, and without feeders birds will spend most of their energy foraging around for food. This is a pivotal time to keep your suet feeders stocked and to hang garlands with fruit and popcorn on your trees. Kids will delight in helping you make homemade treats such as Mockingbird Muffins (see page 67). Throw leftovers such as bread and pancakes out your back door and fill tray and ground feeders with nuts. If snow and ice are hazardous in your area, move the feeders closer to your back door so you can refill them easily and make sure they are free of snow and ice.

Spring

Traffic will begin to increase steadily at your feeders during this time of year as birds begin to migrate to your area. Some backyard visitors will be making a quick pit stop on the way to their final destination, which may result in your seeing a variety of unusual birds you may not see otherwise. That's why it's important to be fully ready with lots of food on hand. Fill your seed feeders to provide for the masses, especially goldfinches. Hang out your hummingbird feeders, mix eggshells in with your homemade treats and seed to provide extra calcium, and offer some fresh water.

Summer

Because of the high abundance of insects and wild fruits in summer, you will see less traffic at your feeders and more in your bushes, beds, trees, and shrubs. However, you will still have some loyal customers, such as sparrows and starlings. Summer is an important time to cut back on seed, relocate your suet feeders to the shade, keep your water feeders clean, and scrub birdbaths so they don't accumulate algae. To provide some added delight for your feathered friends, plant some sunflowers and corn and install a misting sprinkler.

Fall

As in spring, birds are migrating during this season, but this time in the opposite direction. In fact, don't be surprised if you see some of the same birds that graced your feeders in the spring! These hungry travelers need to stock up on some high-energy foods, so it's important to keep your suet feeders stocked and to add some extra feeders around your yard. With fall come pumpkins, gourds, apples, and acorns—all things birds adore. Add diced apple to suet; cut thin slices, dry them in a warm oven, and string onto a garland; or simply set out the cores for the birds to pick on. Dry pumpkin seeds in the oven and pour them into a feeder or set out some pumpkin slices. Use larger gourds to make a feeder (see page 59). Or spend an afternoon gathering acorns in your yard. Put them between wax paper, hammer them open, and set out on platform feeders or mix with suet.

How to Clean Your Feeders . . .

Clean feeders attract more wild birds because the fresh, clean seed is more tempting to their palettes. It's also more nutritious. What's more, dirty feeders can harbor bacteria and spread disease. Here are some tips so you can maintain clean, healthy feeders.

- **Clean on a regular basis:** All feeders should be cleaned at least once a month, but if some feeders in your yard are very popular—that is, you have a large number of birds visiting a particular feeder or two—clean those more often. Hummingbird feeders should be cleaned each time the nectar is refilled (about every two or three days).

- **Use the right cleanser:** One part bleach to nine parts hot water does the job well. Commercial birdfeeder cleaning solutions are also effective, and a mild solution of unscented dish detergent will work just as well.

- **Clean all the parts:** To prevent disease, it is important to clean every part of the feeder, including all feeding ports, perches, lids, platforms, and reservoirs. The feeder's hooks, poles and any other parts where birds may perch or feces may collect should also be cleaned.

- **Use rubber gloves and brushes:** Wear rubber and use stiff brushes so that you can get off feces and sticky seed or suet. Pet-supply stores offer specialized brushes for different sizes and shapes of feeders, but regular bottle brushes are fine too. For hard-to-reach places, use an old toothbrush.

- **Rinse and rinse again:** After cleaning, make sure you rinse everything thoroughly to be sure all chemical residue is removed.

- **Dry completely:** The feeder must be completely dry before refilling with seed. Otherwise, mold and mildew could form, rotting the seed and causing illness.

Garlands galore . . .

When it's time to decorate outdoors for the holidays, don't forget your backyard friends!

Edible garlands

Edible garlands are a wonderful, decorative way to provide food for wild birds. These can hang vertically from branches or be strung around trees or along fences. And there are so many edible things you can use, from day-old donuts to popcorn, peanuts, and dried fruit. Arm yourself with 6-foot lengths of cotton string or dental floss (1-foot for vertical garlands) and a large needle and use your imagination; a garland can be made from just about anything soft enough for a needle to go through. Here are some ideas to get you started:

- walnut halves
- peanuts in the shell
- day-old donuts
- raisins
- dried pasta
- rosehips
- popcorn
- cranberries dipped in lightly beaten egg whites and rolled in sugar
- dried fruit (apples, papaya, oranges, apricots, etc.)
- unsalted pretzels

Birds love natural grasses, berries, cedar, and seed. With some cookie cutters, jelly molds, and wire you can turn your yard into a wonderland of goodies.

Making a grass seed wreath

If you prefer birds to feed in a more natural setting, there's nothing better than a natural grass seed wreath. Not only are they simple to make but they look beautiful gracing a shed door or hanging on a tree, and they make fabulous gifts any time of year.

Some of the most colorful all-natural ingredients you can use in your wreath are sprays of dried sunflower, safflower, thistle, canola, millet, red sorghum, and thistle. For variety, add some Indian corn, dried fruit, ebony wheat, canary grass, amaranth, and rose hips. Wild grapes, purple coneflowers, poppy heads, and wild berries offer additional interest.

To get started, purchase a grapevine wreath, which can be found at a local craft store for a few dollars. Wire a mixture of some of the tall dried grass stems with heads mentioned above, or substitute some wheat, oats, or quaking grass to fill it out.

Once you're finished, hang the wreath outdoors. Don't be surprised if some of the birds also use the materials to build nests!

Gelatin Adornments

Thanks to cookie cutters and cake molds, you can make almost anything out of a little gelatin and seed. To make this wreath, combine ⅓ cup unflavored gelatin, 1½ cups water, and 8 cups of birdseed. Press the mixture into a miniature Bundt cake

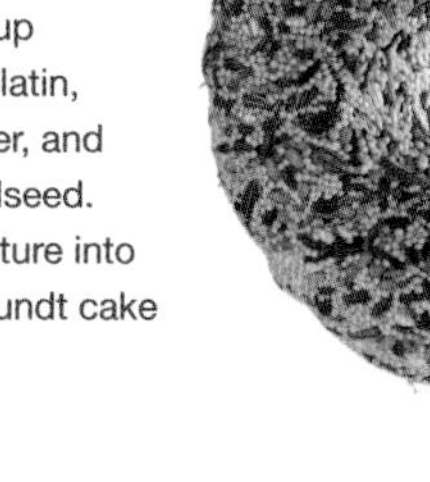

pan or another rounded mold. Refrigerate for 4 hours, then carefully remove from the mold. Let it dry overnight, then decorate it with edibles. Or dress it up with raffia, large accents, ribbon or bows.

To make ornaments, simply spread this gelatin seed mixture onto a cookie sheet, chill, and use cookie cutters to make the shapes. Let dry before hanging outside or wrapping them up for gifts.

A natural holiday garland

If you want to decorate your home for the holidays, why not display something the birds can enjoy afterward? Holly berry and cedar garlands are beautiful adorning a front door. And they are so simple to make—just wire them together into one long string. Once the holidays are over, offer them to your feathered friends. They will love it!